T0308607

Landscape and Journey

POEMS

William Virgil Davis

WINNER OF THE NEW CRITERION POETRY PRIZE

Ivan R. Dee
CHICAGO 2009

*Funding for this year's New Criterion Poetry Prize
has been provided by the Drue Heinz Trust.*

www.ivanrdee.com

Library of Congress Cataloging-in-Publication Data:

Davis, William Virgil, 1940—
    Landscape and journey : poems / William Virgil Davis.
        p. cm. — (Winner of the New Criterion Poetry Prize)
    ISBN: 978-1-56663-839-5 (cloth : alk. paper)
    I. Title.
PS3554.A9383L36 2009
811 '.54—dc22

                    2009033832

For Carol

Contents

I

II

III

Acknowledgments

Grateful acknowledgment is made to the following publications in whose pages many of these poems—some in slightly different versions—first appeared: *Agenda* (UK): "Pomegranates"; *Agni*: "The Other"; *Borderlands* (UK): "First Light"; *The Centennial Review*: "Questions About the *Odyssey*"; *The Chariton Review*: "Those Sunday Mornings," "A Night at the Movies"; *Christianity and Literature*: "Pilgrimage"; *Flyway: A Literary Review*: "A Street Scene"; *The Gettysburg Review*: "A Vision in Late Afternoon," "Geographical," "November," "The Staying," "'Three Dancing Maidens'"; *The Hudson Review*: "October: With Rain," "Tapestry," "The Ohio Poem," "The River: A Vision," "Winter Roses," "Winter Solstice," "What We Said"; *Langdon Review of the Arts in Texas*: "'Border View, Hot Springs, Texas'"; *Mid-American Review*: "In the Cold Air Register"; *The New Criterion*: "A Visit to Manafon," "Courtyard Looking Toward Artemis from the West Cloister," "Landscape," "'Landscape with a Pollard Willow,'" "Poem Ending with a Variation on a Line by Charles Wright"; *PN Review* (UK): "'Red Flowers on Black,'" "Sestina with Two Lines by Charles Tomlinson"; *Poet Lore*: "Something I Cannot Name Has Come Close to Me"; *Poetry*: "Double Elegy" (as "Windows" and "For My Father"); *Prairie Schooner*: "Diet"; *The Sewanee Review*: "Another Pilgrimage," "Ghost," "Ruskin at Brantwood," "Scenes from Childhood"; *Southwest Review*: "Standing Lookout Above Graves End"; *Tar River Poetry*:

"Some Autumn Afternoon"; *TriQuarterly*: "An Affair," "Call"; *Western Humanities Review*: "Stave Church."

"Vigil at Heiligenkreuz" appeared in the chapbook *Winter Light*.

"Landscape," "First Light," "Pilgrimage," and "Standing Lookout above Graves End" appeared in *Other Land: Contemporary Poems on Wales and Welsh-American Experience* (2008).

The author would like to thank the Writers' League of Texas for a fellowship that provided time for work on some of these poems.

I began to assemble and recast anything that still passed
muster in order to re-create before my own eyes . . . the
picture of the landscape, now almost immersed in oblivion,
through which my journey had taken me.

—W. G. Sebald

Landscape and Journey

I

Landscape

How old the dark has become,
standing silent in these fields while
horses weave through each other's shadows.
They have come like warm rain
and run over the hills in the moonlight
and stood so long alone no one
impatient would ever notice them there.

When the wind and the winter return
the horses will still be here,
their silhouettes outlined in the pale moonlight,
standing still and silent on these hills,
or stamping, splattering snow in small spills,
the whole scene turning slowly into landscape
like our own earliest memories.

In the Cold Air Register

Sometimes, when something would fall
into the cold air register, my father
would take me by the legs and lower me
into it. His fingers, locked
like leg irons on my ankles, held me
as I fumbled for what had fallen.
When I'd call, he would pull me,
wet with sweat, my head spinning,
back up into the clear air, into the room
spattered with such bright light.

Those Sunday Mornings

I remember best those Sunday
mornings in winter, with snow
over everything, and the air so
cold it broke like teeth breaking

when I went out to find the
bundles of papers, dust the snow
from them and assemble them,
all the ads added to the center

sections making them extra heavy.
Then to set off along the lanes
of lighted streets, the snow falling
fast, clawing across the light.

I made the same rounds, those
Sunday mornings, that I made
every day, but it took longer,
and it was a harder work.

This was my first experience
with carrying words to people,
but I knew, even then, that it
was what I'd always want to do.

The Ohio Poem

for James Wright

1

It is early morning.
Trees lift from the fog the sun
is burning away.
Along the river the Iroquis called beautiful
an Indian stalks the faint imprint
of a twelve-point buck
who moves off ahead of him downwind.

2

I remember the thicket,
the hobo jungle,
where the park ended at the railroad tracks.

Once I touched on old bum
I thought was dead.
When he sat up
I ran the whole way
home,

too terrified to tell
where I had been.

One spring my brother and I
met one of them
at the top of the hill.
He waved and spoke to us.

That afternoon we saw him again.
He was leaning against a tree
near the small stream at the bottom of the hill.
His face was clean. His head rested
lightly against the tree.

He seemed to be asleep.
Unless you looked closely
you would never see
the bracelets of blood he wore.

Later, we tried to remember:
did we speak,
or slip past silent?

3

And now your bones are turning
dark, like emeralds,
burning in the dark wind
somewhere along the dirty Ohio north of Wheeling,
where the women dry their wings.

Gentleman Jim, are you gone?

Winter Solstice

A pink wash over everything
and the wind down to whisper.
Squirrels stop on bare branches
and blend in so quickly if you look
away you never find them again.

This twilight must happen only
here, only once or twice each year.
I saw it first last winter, black
trees and houses lined up along
the horizon like silhouettes cut

out of paper and set up along
a board in a classroom long gone
into memory, where I first stared
at the shapes light makes on things
and learned I wanted to repeat them

Scenes from Childhood

1

In winter, when a dirty lace
of snow wristed the walks and driveways,
the coalman came. His truck
shiny black, he backed in
from the back alley, slid his chute through
the basement window and shoveled
the coal into the cellar. For a few
minutes there was nothing in the world
but the rumble of the coal coming in
and the black dust filling the air.

2

We would hear the horses before
we saw them. And then the wagon rounded
the corner, its pear-shaped bell
ringing with the jerking motion.
The horses started and stopped,
snorted and pawed the street, flipping
their heads and manes, switching their tails.
The bread was always warm.
The breadman carried the loaves

lined up along his arm like a litter of sleeping kittens.
Even after the wagon was long gone,
the neighborhood was permeated by
the sweet smell of fresh bread.

3

The ice, covered with a black tarp
and nested in straw, was cut in huge blocks.
The iceman heaved each block onto his
shoulder like a sack of oats, bending under
its weight. His shiny leather shoulder patch,
strapped over his shirt, gleamed, slippery
with wet. He had a wide gap-toothed
grin and joked with everyone. He put
a block of ice in the icebox in the corner
of the kitchen and, snapping his pincers
at us, laughed his way back to his wagon.
In summer he always gave us slivers to hold
in our mouths. We shivered, loving the cold.

4

He limped along the street, his small
bell ringing with his awkward motion
and the uneven pavement. The women
hurried to find their knives and scissors
and ran to wait along the curb, gossiping
with one another about the weather
and their husbands' work, wondering
about the war and what would become

of it and them. The old man bent beneath
his work and rarely spoke, but the sparks
flew and fell like fountains around his feet.
After he had finished with them,
the knives and scissors were sharp and clean.

Double Elegy

Windows

for my mother, in memory

This small window. I remember my mother,
framed by buds, her breath held, looking for me
in the top of the tree, higher than the house.
We waved and she waited, watching me climb down
through the intricate branches of the old maple
that stood guard at the corner of our yard.

Today I stare, almost level, into scrub oak,
some cedar mixed in, this window years away.
These are the holidays. I imagine my mother
back there, at her window again, watching. What
do we know? Although the seasons have changed
their windows, we watch together. We wave.

For My Father

in memory

I seem to see him often, at dusk, out
near the end of the yard, walking quietly,
alone, into the evening. I watched him

walking there for years before the image
fixed in my mind, became what I knew
I could never forget. Now that he is dead,

his image (something that may be nothing
more than the darkness moving slowly off
at the end of the yard, or coming, slowly,

to meet me) is all that I have left of him.

A Vision in Late Afternoon

The heat like a hand presses against my head,
and I think I see, from across the yard, my mother,

dead, move past the window of the living room.
Obviously in a hurry about something inside,
she'd only glanced quickly out the window
as she passed through the room and then was gone.

This all happened suddenly, as visions always do.
But now I wonder if my mother might have seen me,
fleetingly, standing there in the yard, as she hurried
through the room. Was she, like me, unsure of what

she thought she saw? Was it too late for her to turn,
to look back over her shoulder? I wonder if my image
materialized for her only after she had already gone on
into the other room—in much the same way that my

vision of her flared and burned, then blurred, in the late
afternoon heat, with the weight of all the years.

October: With Rain

The way the light lasts longest on a single spot
of windowpane, some small distortion in the glass
that keeps its final clasp of wind and rain as well,
has caught my eye again. My son has grown so fast
toward man I marvel my own age, try to sort out all
the years, run the film as far forward as I dare.
We sit together at the table, this wintry day
with rain, and do not speak, although I think we think
the same things out, muse on the rain and windowpane,
and in our own ways try to fill the final outline in.

The River: A Vision

for my son

What I saw was a river, a certain slant
of light cut through large leafless trees
bent almost double. That and not much more.
The dark river moved. The wind dropped off
and the trees bent back upright. The sky
blackened and stars appeared. We walked hand
in hand without speaking toward something
in the distance. I don't know what it was
or whether we reached it. That didn't make
much difference. What did seem important
was the river, old symbol for the stream
of time, running swift and dark beneath the
star-struck sky. But this was just a vision.
Why I would want to tell you anything so
indistinct is not clear, even to me. We both
know that I have been wrong about many things.

Vigil at Heiligenkreuz

The cold comes close around us,
breathes with me.
Do I drowse? In the corner,
near the cracked column,
a young monk slips past so quickly
I almost miss him.
He is late, hurrying to service
with his brothers.
He does not think to look
over his shoulder,
never would have noticed me
sitting half-asleep in the long dark
down the cold aisle
of the centuries
where we both serve.

Stave Church

Bygdøy (Oslo)

Even then it must have seemed out of place.
Today, we make our slow wet way up a steep
trail, through evergreens as old as this century,
to a door so low we have almost to bow
to enter. Inside, the air is thick with age.
The dark light does little to illuminate
the small round room, the central wooden
altar, the benches built into the walls.
It is almost impossible to imagine what
it must have been like: the small crowd
congregated here no more than once or twice
a year, sitting without speech in this place
made holy by tradition more than anything
else. We sit and stare and hug ourselves
for warmth. It has the hush of churches
anywhere and I wonder that we make so many
pilgrimages to places like this, often almost
inaccessible, to sit and stare off into
the musty ancient air of other centuries.
What do we hope to find? Our faint faith,
our little service ended, we rise and bend
beneath the door again and track our way

back the way we came, through a snowy trail
of our own faintly frozen footprints.

A Visit to Manafon

for R. S. Thomas

Still patches of snow on the high hills
above this frost valley where new lambs
run from watching ewes in air so cold
with chill your breath like glassy mirrors
breaks off in front of you and you walk
through your own reflection—think back
through time to more than forty years ago.

•

The small chapel, built from stone quarried
from the nearby river, has stood for centuries.
The western wall, thick with vine-veined
stone, is a map of the rooted land itself.
In the tiny room at the back of the nave
two small windows—barred since recent
break-ins—hold fifteenth century angels

in pale green and yellow glass. The warden,
from her lambing fields, aproned in mud,
has come to let us in. She watches nonchalantly
as we roam around. There isn't much to see.
"We sometimes have a dozen for services." She

identifies herself as she would be remembered,
"The little girl in the blue dress," and gives

her maiden name to those, like us, who ask
about the past. The great man, when he was here,
we wondered, did she remember him? "Oh,
yes, of course. How could I ever forget? It's all,
now, that brings folks like you. Nothing else.
Yes, he was here for twelve years. He sometimes
came out to the fields when we were bringing

in the hay." "To help?" "Yes," she laughed,
"to help. But he was such a big, strong man.
He threw the hay all the way over the wagon.
Mostly, though, he came at night, to sit and talk
before our kitchen fires. He had a gentle voice,
always spoke softly. But the eyes. That's what
you'd remember, the eyes, like fire reflected;

burning, always burning." We take a quick last
look, sign the book, thank her for opening, then
wander out into the walled grounds, the small
cemetery surrounding the church, through patches
of snowdrops, down the short curve of road, past
the ash tree that unleaved suddenly like a fountain,
to the rectory (now in private hands) beside the river.

•

All is still. Everything is damp. The trees drip.
The hills surround this spot, this hushed hollow.
We have no time to climb above the village,
see from where he saw the rolling hills of Wales

stretch westward toward the sea. It is as if the silence itself has spoken. Below, the people he came here to serve; above, his distanced God.

Tapestry

Veins and arteries carry the blood from corner
to corner. The interpretation is easy once you find
the right place to begin. The Duke, on his white
stallion, has killed a knight from the invading
army near the center of the scene. Three of his
own followers lie in a heap at his feet. There are
too many corpses to count. A small stream winds
through the valleys, the rolling hills of the
background, done in a flourish of autumnal color.
In the lower left-hand corner, worked intricately
into the dense undergrowth, is the small signature
of one of the women who worked her life away
on the other side of this scene, in the cold tower
where the tapestry, for centuries, has hung.

An Ordinary Day

He is standing with his feet in fire.
The wind whips his hair around his head.
His arms are tied behind his back.

The crowd is watching, waiting for him
to scream—for the spectacle to begin.
If he stands very still, and stares straight

forward, and is silent, they will be
disappointed. Later, if anyone ever asks
about this day, no one will remember

his name. They will remember only
the way the wind fanned the flames
and how the fire feathered high and hot

and curled quick and close about him
like a burning blanket, and that he closed
his eyes, and did not cry out. They will say

that the day was only an ordinary one.

Some Autumn Afternoon

Almost imperceptibly, the wind has begun
to turn the early evenings into words like
sweater, roaring fire, brandied pears, quilts.
All along the streets, trees bend and sway,
wanting winter's simplicity, the snow's soft hug.

The whole landscape holds like mirrors,
like months of disciplined thought, the mind
alert to the least hint of emotion or memory,
ready already to turn in on itself, to work
everything out, the way the seasons have.

By late afternoon, the streets are deserted.
The houses, as solitary as cats, hunch and watch.
Windows blaze with red and orange along
the western façades. Dust devils sweep the streets
and disappear into thin air. The huge sycamore

on the corner has started to shed its shingles
of rough bark. The oaks and maples blush red
and orange, waving their leaves away. Rivers
of smoke meander above the houses and whole
acres of air have turned ashen. Everything

hesitates. Each year, some autumn afternoon, there is this slight shudder, a bird through barren branches, a dog's distant bark, this pause on the way home, when the scene seems to fix like a photograph, suspended in memory.

II

"Landscape with a Pollard Willow"

—Hanns Lautensack

The telescoped view
forces the focus through
the foliage, the fingering
limbs, leaving the gaze to linger

on the church, its tower and steeple,
fixed in the center of the scene.
There are no people to be seen,
no animals. There is simply

this scope of the land, etched
as it might have been sketched
on an afternoon walk by one
on his long way home alone.

Winter Roses

November: the cold walks stark
in sunlight; the whole hillside
filled with snow. On the small
balcony, you stand and stare.
Your coffee cools in the tiny
china cup beside the marble
balustrade where winter roses
bloom in heated glass containers.
The fragile curtains frost
with fresh designs. It is all
years ago now. You stand alone
and see how unobtrusively
the dark fills up the dark.

Pomegranates

The blood-red arils, tart to the tongue,
slash the thirsty throats of history, and men
along long trails and over mountains,
slog through sand as deep as camels' knees
and, whipped by winter's winds, are now
about to turn the corner of another century
somewhere in the deserts of Afghanistan.

Pomegranates cluster close against the house,
near the back door that bangs behind you
as you enter a room of ghosts—who never
fail to recognize you in spite of your ever
more elaborate disguises. The thick-skinned,
several-celled berries brush their reflections
in the windows. We are all eating glass.

Geographical

A tiger drinks from a pool of water
in the midst of a meadow surrounded
by meadows and a few trees, somewhere

in Africa or India, it doesn't matter.
The wind blows the long grasses, making
the tiger almost invisible, making the place

a place we can imagine, a place where we
could walk and watch, a place where
we might even drink from such a still

pool of water and raise our eyes, as the tiger
has just done, and look long at something
in the distant distance, or into the wind,

and hesitate for a moment, as the tiger has,
before he bends to drink again, before he
disappears as quickly and as quietly as he

came, into those softly blowing trees,
those long greeny grasses, his eyes alert
to every possible danger as he moves

slowly and cautiously away, leaving
this unstirred pool, these stopped trees,
to us, here in deepest India or Africa.

"Three Dancing Maidens"

In Central Park three maidens dance.
They're holding hands, or trying to.
The one in the middle has a shawl

draped over her outstretched
arms, one foot kicked off the ground.
She could almost fall. Although

the fountain has not yet been turned
on, and the tulip display must wait
for early May, their flowing dresses

wetly cling tightly to their bodies,
then fall free and flap between their legs
and knees. They look at one another,

laughing, barefoot and oblivious,
with all their breasts exposed. No one
is there to see them except one young

couple on a bench behind — and me,
more than a thousand miles away,
seeing them in the *New York Times*,

in the story about the burst of spring
come early this year after a long cold
winter. The caption reads, "A Cold

Snap, and a Warm Solution," and calls
the bronzed maidens' dance a "revel."
I wonder what it does reveal about

New York, or them, or any of us?
The background is barren and dead
although the hedge behind the girls

is green, perhaps permanently so.
The cuddling couple are covered
with a yellow blanket, but more

wrapped up in themselves. He's
kissing her on the side of her head.
She seems to have her eyes closed,

unaware of the dance being performed
as if just for them. She has her feet set
firmly on the ground, but he has bent

her over on his lap (it looks uncomfortable),
and both their heads are cowled in
the yellow blanket. But then I see,

beneath the feet of the far right
dancer, one wheel and part of what
could be a stroller, parked close

beside their bench. Is there a child
in it? If so, would that change anything,
insist on a different interpretation?

What do we ever know about such
scenes, such circumstances? Even
Walter Schott's bronze maidens may

be deceiving us, may be deceived
about themselves, or what they are
about, that we have seen them so.

Poem Ending with a Variation on a Line by Charles Wright

Winter, and sleeves of grey bone hang limp in
the wind. The tortured sun has cut its own throat.
This late in this late century nothing is new

or news. We nod off in the early afternoons
and wake, unrested, to icy feet and fevers.
Under their snowy hill, out of the wind at last,

my parents continue to repeat their prayers
in the same ways that we, with our raspy throats,
try to comfort one another. How many days

have disappeared into dark tunnels? How many
times will we come back to empty cupboards
and drained drinks, to landscape like laundry

frozen on a line? In a bare corner of an empty
room an old spider has spun an awkward web.
The distance between the living and the dead

is no more than one heartbeat or one breath.

A Street Scene

When I think of seeing them, walking
down the street, hand in hand, the woman
and the little boy, no doubt her son,
why do I associate this scene, this street
of spring at dusk somewhere in Ohio,
with this strange unrest I feel now,
more than thirty years later? Why do I
let that distant light remind me of, not
something that has passed by long ago,
but something that still lies ahead,
something I do not now know and have
no way of knowing?

                They were walking
away from me. I never saw their faces.
They did not seem to speak. The woman's
dress, cut loose around her knees, swayed
softly as she walked. They entered the tunnel
of trees. The small boy had to stretch to hold
her hand. He rather bounced along beside her.
Occasionally, he looked up at her and she
looked down at him, but I don't think they
talked. Once or twice, before they passed
from view, they seemed to swing their joined

hands in a little half-arc, and, once,
I'm certain, I saw the small boy skip.

Sestina with Two Lines by Charles Tomlinson

Summer thunder darkens: the evening is falling apart.
It is the end of the end of the second season of the year.
We have lived through the apocalypse for too long.
The last doubled rainbow has fallen out of the sky.
Sheep on the rambling hills are eating their lives away.
All the roads in are narrow and filled with potholes.

Once off of the main road we confronted the potholes,
so many that we wondered if the car would fall apart
before we arrived. For years now we had been away,
but we had almost forgotten the intervening years
as we sat there over a cold dinner watching the sky
gather into the thunderstorm, wondering how long

it might be before we could go out again. Not long,
as it turned out. So we drove back through the potholes
and into the shabby town, and watched the darkening sky
glimpse gold and red before the last clouds parted
and everything suddenly went to full dark, like the years
we could hardly remember, the years we had been away.

We took a drink in a small smoky pub but went away
before the loud crowd came. After that it wasn't long
until we were on the road again (now how like the years
it seemed) making our slow way back through the potholes

to the small lonely house. Still, we knew it was all part
of something we had seen fleetingly in the dark sky.

When we arrived back, there was nothing left of sky.
The whole landscape seemed to have gone far away.
We climbed up to our room, acting our proper parts,
without speaking, and I wondered if you were longing
to get away again, even if we had to deal with potholes,
even if we didn't know where to go with the years

left to us. I guess we both knew by then that the years
would be shorter, and that even the most spectacular sky
was short-lived and filled with its own kind of potholes,
and that, no matter how we tried, there was no way,
really, to get away, no matter the miles and the longing,
no matter the weather; and that we all had our parts

to play, and that all the parts were filled with potholes,
and no matter how long we waited, how many years,
a dark sky would lead us on; that there was no other way.

Ruskin at Brantwood

(toward the end)

The stone chair in the woods
faces the small waterfall, its back
to the sharp drop of the hill
down to the house, high above
the calm Coniston waters.

He sits and thinks of the waters
of Venice, strung out as streets;
of the *Lamps of Architecture* and
Modern Painters, two of his old
obsessions; of his lovely Effie
with his friendly enemy Millais.

Rocking himself slowly to sleep
in the ferny Turner twilight,
he dreams and muses, ghost-
guessing the encroaching presence
of his own absence, the full dark.

Ghost

How easy it is to make a ghost.
—Keith Douglas

My man and shadow meet
before me on the ground.
The world is all elsewhere.
We stare and stare, then calmly
look around. There is no sound.

This ghost grown from my feet
leads softly into earth. We turn and
turn together, lean hard on one
another to learn the line that separates
us, but keeps us firmly bound.

First Light

for R. S. Thomas (in memory)

I climb the steep stone
steps, glassy with cold,
to enter the empty church.
Faint light swords through
the upper dark. No wind
murmurs. No candles burn.
No God waits there nor wakes.

Last night, quite abruptly,
it began to rain. And then,
before morning, the rain
turned slowly to snow. And
then again, before first
light, almost imperceptibly,
the snow turned back to rain.

A Night at the Movies

The film already fifteen minutes old,
their awkward line was ushered in by hand.
I wonder what it was that they'd been told?

They stumbled down the aisle as shy and bold
as children lined in lines, hands held in hands —
the film already fifteen minutes old.

Their leader led them to the front and scolded
them to sit and stare and try to understand.
I wondered what it was that they'd been told?

And then one old man, out of all control,
stood, and started to talk—to comprehend—
the film already fifteen minutes old.

Five minutes later, still staring over their shoulders,
their leader led them out, held hand in hand.
I wonder what it was that they were told?

Since then this scene has folded and unfolded
again and again in the darkened room of my mind.
The film is always fifteen minutes old.
I wonder what it was that they were told?

Questions about the Odyssey

Knowing what she knew, could she
have waited so long, faithfully weaving
the years away by day, tearing them out

(the way one tears hair out we'd think)
each evening? And could they, the suitors,
be imagined to be so gullible? Would any

man not wonder, waiting that way,
what would be left to him, after all? Or,
are we to imagine it all differently—

since the main action (until the end)
is all elsewhere, with Odysseus and his men,
who take their own good time coming home?

What does Homer intend for us to do
with this story anyhow? What are we to say
about it, when we finish? Does literature

reflect life? Is life an odyssey? Does
it make any difference if Penelope is true,
or if Odysseus finally does come home?

"Red Flowers on Black"

(after a painting by Elizabeth Bishop)

Elizabeth Bishop's Devil's Paintbrush bouquet
sprouts out of thin air, from a fourteen-fingered
fist of leaves. The red heads bud on the flat black
background and nod in conversation like old
straight-laced ladies. Several, in small groups
of three or more, lean their heads together
or half turn away to whisper over their shoulders.
One seems about to wander away into another
room off-right to think it all over, or to say quietly
something she's been thinking about for years.

Standing Lookout above Graves End

Tonight the sea is calm. There is no wind.
Invent the wind. From this high cliff the rocks
beneath the rocks cluster like herds of ancient
creatures gone to stone. Nothing, now, moves
them save the sea which moves nothing. Invent
the wind. Do not stand here only to stare.
Invent the wind and let it stream through
these dead lungs, these gills gone out of use.
Invent the wind. Invent, invent, invent the wind.

Courtyard Looking Toward Artemis from the West Cloister

—Isabella Stewart Gardner Museum, Boston

Unarmed Artemis, your mouth
opened in awe or slight surprise,
you stand surveying the scene in

this most modern garden. Centuries
spin before your sightless eyes while lilies
ring their silent bells. Frail ferns

and cineraria whisper softly
in the stone-stilled atmosphere.
We wander among the squared-off

rooms surrounding you, turning
over in our minds thoughts we thought
we had forgotten. Each turn brings

back to breath the beautiful,
the true. Then we return to you.
Demetrius of Ephesus, your fears

have proven false. We stand and stare,
and wonder if, in our modern world,
when we return to it, our being here

and seeing you will make much
difference. We walk out into the world
to do what we must do.

Poem Beginning and Ending with a Variation of a Line by Geoffrey Hill

I stray amid the things that will not stay.
I look at you and watch you look away.

It seems that we've both been here before,
although we can't remember when. On the shore

three gulls eye us warily, then haughtily stalk
off. We have given up even on small talk.

We climb the steep path, through stepped sand,
to the ruined castle. In the keep we take our last stand

and stare out over sunset-ribboned water. All day
we've strayed amid things that we know won't stay.

III

Something I Cannot Name Has Come Close to Me

In deep waters blind fish struggle
toward lines not yet let down.

November

And has it now come to this, this
autumn room, this sitting in silence,
waiting for whatever it is to arrive,

to this certain uncertainty? The light
opens the window and bars me in.
Even the words on a page, read

relevantly, read slowly. Although
I remember much, some things,
now, seem difficult to remember.

I must trust that all that needs recall,
I will recall. It is almost noon. I am
waiting for someone to arrive. He is late,

but I have always been patient,
and so I will wait, watch the long
afternoon shortening its shadows,

listen to the few birds singing,
the old clock ticking, see the last
leaves flutter from the stoic trees.

Pilgrimage

We never knew the way, couldn't get there
for the going. All day the sky had been grey
with a light mist falling. Not knowing what

we were looking for or finding had found,
we were anxious to finish whatever it was
we'd begun, to have this day put away,

on the calendar, in the album, where if we
wanted to we could take it out later and
examine it—fixed, unchanged, framed,

defined, a piece of history, even if our own.
It comes to this: we choose the life we live.
For years now I have been carrying one

small smooth stone to a nameless shrine.

Another Pilgrimage

—Bardsey Island, off the coast of Wales

The dead are climbing slowly
up the steep hill from the old
stone church, crouched close
below, and often washed by water,
as in ancient tide-told times.

•

We walk, today, the way
those ghostly pilgrims of the past
streamed along these hills,
along this long length of land
within sight of the sanctuary
they sought, which, if cheaper
than Rome, was twice the trouble.

Across four treacherous
kilometers of roughly wrinkled
water, the ship-like shape
of the island rears up in mist
and rain, staring at those
who stare, those who've come
to stop and rest and pray.

•

Done, we turn to return,
winding our long slow way
back up, over these holy hills,
passing again the faithful dead,
coming eternally down.

Diet

I wonder what you must have been like
at sixteen or seventeen—beautiful,
no doubt, but even then (those terrified eyes)

afraid of what you knew you didn't
know, of what you guessed and what
you kept at bay—the way you kept

the boys away by asking them to come
close, come closer. It is still all there
in your eyes, but I am old enough to know

such tricks, the way you've teased life
itself into a corner, like a cat a mouse,
playing with it—thinking at any time

you could end the game any way you
wanted. You ate words for the sake
of poems and swallowed them so hard

it hurt to watch. Now you have grown
thin. You take a cracker or two for lunch,
nibble several bites for dinner. We never

talk of anything edible. You wear the
same suit you wore thirty years ago,
the day I first saw you—all in black

in a stark white room, reading with such
a hush we all held our breath. Your words
echoed in our heads as if they were our own.

But, then and now, you never noticed
us, or anyone else. Now, I want to say
gorge yourself, my dear. Get up

in the middle of the night and raid
the refrigerator. Go out for an early
breakfast. Have a large lunch at a deli.

Do this every day, for weeks, months.
Eat. Eat everything. Do not let me hear
from you again until you are fat—

you who have always been famous
for your metaphors of starvation.

Call

You know, she said,
he used to call me
maybe six or seven
times a day, interrupt-
ing anything I was
doing, he didn't care,
and it was always
something small he
wanted, to ask a
question or to tell me
something he was
thinking about, or
what he had heard
on the radio he
listened to all day
long, and I got angry
with him often and
once I even said
I didn't want to hear
about it, or from him,
again, I'm tired, I said,
of listening to what
you want to tell me,
why don't you do
something, or call

somebody else,
even though I knew
he had no one else,
and that he often
called me because
of that, that he was
lonely, although
he never said so,
it wasn't his way,
maybe he didn't even
know it himself, or
think about it that
way, it made me
wonder, and I do
wonder what he
did all day long,
sitting there in his
chair, all alone,
listening to the radio,
and maybe thinking
how he might call
me, just to hear
a live voice, just
to talk back to
somebody, and
then maybe he'd
think he shouldn't
call again so soon,
and then wonder
when he had called
the last time, and
not know for sure,
and put his hand

on the phone and
almost dial the full
number, and then
put the receiver
back on the hook
and plan to wait
at least another
hour and then,
when he did call,
he must have heard
the disappointment
in my voice and
maybe he even
imagined all kinds
of things about
himself, or me,
and wondered,
when I told him
I had things to do,
or somewhere to
go, whether I was
telling him the truth,
because he knew
what my life was
like, that I didn't
do very much,
and rarely even left
the house myself,
but we never talked
about that, we never
really talked about
much of anything,
we talked talk, and

then we hung up,
often with some
excuse neither
of us believed in,
and now, every
day, I sit here
alone, and I wish
he would call.

The Other

If he'd known she was watching
from the window in the building
across the street he might not
have been so nonchalant with
the waiter or have waited until
the entrée arrived to take her hand
in his and place it on the gloves
he had given her the week before,
a gift he still had no real knowledge
of with respect to her deepest
feelings about them because she
so seldom said exactly what she
felt about anything. This, he thought,
was one of the major differences
between the woman across the table
from him and the other one.

As he thought of her he turned to
glance out of the window—almost
as if he'd felt a pair of eyes on him,
warming his face the way his hand
was growing warm as he and she sat
staring at each other over a fancy
dessert neither of them really wanted
but both had ordered because they

each thought the other did, and as
the light in the window, darkening,
seemed to signal a turn, like the turning
on of lights within a room, or all along
the street outside the window, or
in the windows all along the street.

What We Said

There wasn't any way to know
most of it for sure, and it wouldn't
have made much difference anyhow.
So what we said, the way we told
it, was as good as any, since truth
can't ever really be found out or
untangled, the rope finally thrown
away with the knot still in it. So
what we said was that she must
have known him, must have let
him in because there wasn't any
sign of forced entry, no broken
windows, and the only door locked
from the inside. He wasn't some
sort of magician or shape-changer
who could slip in through the chimney
or come in under the door like
smoke or empty air, appear or
disappear at will. He probably sat
there talking to her for a while,
and she might even have given him
something to drink because there
were two glasses in the sink, and
two cups too, but, without fingerprints,
it will be difficult to know anything

for certain. Maybe the autopsy will
tell us what she had to eat or drink,
and maybe not, if it was only liquid.
Anyhow, they must have walked
to the bedroom together, even if
she'd had too much to drink, and
she'd folded some of her clothes,
as if she was waiting for him, or,
maybe, that was when he came
in, interrupting her while she was
undressing, after waiting, watching
her from the window over the fire
escape, the one window unlocked
and still open a crack when we arrived.
So what we thought was that there
might be fingerprints on the window
sill or somewhere else in the room,
or on one of the glasses in the sink,
or somewhere where we least
expected them, but we didn't find
any prints anywhere — other than
hers which, of course, were everywhere.
Her eyes were open, a beautiful
blue, and she looked only slightly
startled to be staring so, as if she'd
been surprised by death too, or
hadn't expected it, or only seen it
coming when he came too close,
and she probably thinking of
something else, something totally
different, and only then, at the last
instant, saw it for what it was,
and saw it was too late, and maybe

she started to smile at that, realizing,
and then stopped, just as she died.
So what we said was that it looked
like love gone wrong, a real accident,
something totally unintended.
Still, she had only been in the city
several weeks and as far as we
knew she hadn't found a job or
had much time to make new
acquaintances or find friends,
and we know she hadn't known
anyone here before, in another life
so to speak, someone who might
have been watching or waiting
for her, someone who had followed
her home, a secret admirer,
or even a former friend she'd be
happy to see when he arrived,
even unexpectedly—someone she
would have welcomed in to talk
about the past they had had together,
or the place they both were from,
or to catch up on old news. We
knew that, most likely, many
of the things we imagined were
things we would never be able
to prove, that most cases of this kind
are never solved. But we always
try to do our best, and, therefore,
if anybody asks, you can tell him
that this is what we said.

An Affair

When he discovered it
he discovered almost
immediately that everybody
already knew about it.
But nobody had told
him — not surprisingly,
he thought. He knew
he would not have told
anyone either, if he'd
known about something
like this, not even his
best friend, not even his
wife. Indeed, he wondered
how one, really, *would*
go about talking about it?
In this case, wouldn't it
be obvious that (if not
everyone) some at least
would have already
known and, therefore, it
would seem that they
would have assumed
that he knew too — and
thus not tell him — because
(they'd also assume)

either that he knew—
and was trying to ignore it—
or, if he didn't, that he
wouldn't *want* to be told?
They must all, he thought,
have thought that he knew,
thought that he was being
adult about it (not, surely,
that he didn't care, but
just that he didn't care
to discuss it). Even she,
he thought, must have
thought he knew, since—
after the first few months—
she never made any attempt
to hide it from him. Even
so, she must have wondered,
as time went on, when *he*
might mention it, how he
might bring it up, under
what circumstances, where
they might be at the time.
Knowing him, she imagined,
if he *were* to bring it up, it
would, inevitably, be at the
most unlikely moment,
and under the most awkward
circumstances. Early on,
she'd even thought about
what she would say, how
she would defend herself,
even if she would deny it all
outright (in spite of all the

obvious, incriminating,
evidence), or—if she'd been
caught off-guard—might
attempt to throw the blame
back on him, accuse him
of having forced her into it
(even subconsciously)
for some sort of strange
psychological need
he had, and had,
perhaps, repressed.

But, as time went on,
and he didn't say, or do,
anything, and because she
couldn't really be certain
that he really didn't know—
unlikely as such an assumption
was—she stopped thinking
of possible excuses, stopped
inventing various, almost
plausible, scenarios to
cover herself, or even, she
thought, to *protect him*—
if it came to that. And,
therefore, the new became
old all over again, became
a justification for both
of them: he, waiting for her
to get bored with her lover
and come back to him,
to confess—contritely,
he hoped—and be forgiven,

so that they could make
up, and take up where
they had left off; she,
for him to say something,
do something, take some
sort of action, hint at least
that he knew—or, at least,
suspected something—
even, she thought, take
up with another woman,
and thus give her both
an excuse for continuing,
something to throw up
to him—if it ever did
come out and she needed
(as she knew she might)
some excuse. But both
of them, no doubt, knew
that neither would do
either—or both both.

One of the things, finally,
that most intrigued him
was the way he had,
apparently, *permitted* it all
to happen, the way he
had pretended to himself
that it wasn't really
happening at all, that
she was not away,
so many days, on some
trumped up trip, but
actually upstairs, in bed,

asleep, or, even, waiting
for him to come in and
surprise her—even to
make love to her. Had she
noticed, he wondered,
how often he had,
apparently purposely,
chosen to miss something,
overlook an obvious
clue left unaccountably
behind, failed to initiate
a comment or make an
accusation when there
seemed to be an obvious
opening or an
unaccountable gap in
one of her accounts (an
hour or two here or there
left out and open to
question), when she had
given him an almost open
invitation. It was as if,
she thought, that he had
almost *forced* himself
to be deceived—even
as if he wanted to be
finally.

       They had,
of course, both thought
it all through many times,
and they had both come,
independently, to the
same conclusions, again

and again, so that all that
ever surprised either of them
now was that they couldn't
seem to get back to
any kind of beginning
beyond this end.

The Staying

At the last minute, we'd decided to go.
Then, just as we came into view of the harbor,
the boat eased into the current. Everyone
on board was waving. Small flags fluttered.
The men wore white hats and the women
wore white gowns. Some held small white
umbrellas above their heads. We watched
them disappear into the dark and turned
back to return to the hotel, to watch the rain
from windows, to dress for dinner. Later,
we will sit in the lobby with the others
(all of us dressed as if we are ready to go),
sit and stare and then repeat again all
the reasons we can think of for staying,
those for leaving, the way we commiserated
over it for days before making our decisions,
even then, when we knew it was already
too late, that the boat had already begun
to ease away from the dock, from everything
—we will now confess—we always knew
we could never really leave.

"Border View, Hot Springs, Texas"

for Don Neyhard

The house no longer exists.
The outline of a galloping horse
to the right of the doubled
window without glass, the
fist-sized hole just ahead
of the horse's head, are all
long gone. This window into
another world—these hills,
the small white stucco house
in the distance, stunned by sun
and overhung by fog or mist,
floats into my vacant room
of mind to remind me that
everything can quite suddenly
disappear into landscape.

William Virgil Davis is the author of three books of poetry, including *One Way to Reconstruct the Scene* (1980), which won the Yale Series of Younger Poets Award in 1979, and, most recently, *Winter Light* (1990). His critical works include *R. S. Thomas: Poetry and Theology* (2007). He is a professor of English and Writer-in-Residence at Baylor University.